Celebrating your year

1950

a very special year for

A message from the author:

Welcome to the year 1950.

I trust you will enjoy this fascinating romp down memory lane.

And when you have reached the end of the book, please join me in the battle against AI generated copy-cat books and fake reviews.

Details are near the back of the book.

Best regards,
Bernard Bradforsand-Tyler.

Contents

1950 American Family Life	8
Austerity in the United Kingdom	13
Our Love Affair with Automobiles	16
The Golden Age of Television	20
Most Popular TV Shows of 1950	21
Peanuts Comic Strip Debut	24
World's First Credit Card	27
Soviet Propaganda Posters	28
The Cold War—Nuclear Arms Race	29
North Korea Invades South Korea	30
South African Apartheid Laws	34
India—A Country is Born	36
The Great Brink's Robbery	37
Marlon Brando Silver Screen Debut	40
1950 in Cinema and Film	42
Top Grossing Films of the Year	43
1950 Cold War Inspired Films	44
Guys and Dolls Hits Broadway	46
The Lion, the Witch and the Wardrobe	47
Musical Memories	49
1950 Billboard Top 30 Songs	50
Fashion Trends of the 1950s	53
The 4th British Empire Games	62
First FIA World Championship	63
Other Sporting Events	66
Other News from 1950	68
Famous People Born in 1950	72
1950 in Numbers	76
Image Attributions	84

Advertisement

First flight or fiftieth, you'll be glad you chose TWA

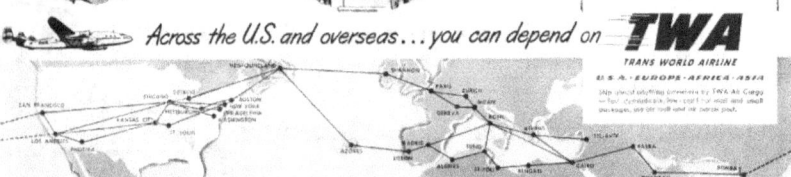

First flight or fiftieth, you'll be glad you chose TWA

Don't look for just *one* reason why more than a million passengers a year fly TWA. For it's not *routes* alone, or *speed* alone, or *service* alone, or *dependability* alone that leads to such loyalty. It's the happy combination of all these factors that makes one airline stand out.

TWA is the only U.S. airline connecting 56 U.S. cities with key points in Europe, Africa and Asia. TWA's speed is unsurpassed. TWA's magnificent Constellations are world-proved for both dependability and comfort.

But the real "plus" is TWA's PEOPLE. Million-mile Flight Captains, courteous, capable hostesses, skilled maintenance helpers all are part of TWA's smoothly functioning team of thousands working together to make your trip fast, comfortable, safe.

Did you know that TWA hostesses are specially trained and equipped to help mothers care for babies... with diapers, bottles, and a kit of supplies?

Let's flashback to 1950, a very special year.

Was this the year you were born?

Was this the year you were married?

Whatever the reason, this book is a celebration of your year,

THE YEAR 1950.

Turn the pages to discover a book packed with fun-filled fabulous facts. We look at the people, the places, the politics and the pleasures that made 1950 unique and helped shape the world we know today.

So get your time-travel suit on, and enjoy this trip down memory lane, to rediscover what life was like, back in the year 1950.

1950 American Family Life

Imagine if time-travel was a reality, and one fine morning you wake up to find yourself flashed back in time, back to the year 1950.

What would life be like for a typical family, in a typical town, somewhere in America?

A family cooling off outside their home in the 1950s.

The post-war boom gave us booming birth numbers, booming suburbs, a booming economy, and the booming trappings of the consumerist culture we still enjoy today. With the stringent post-war years well behind us, the rising middle classes were feeling an urgent need to spend.

An unprecedented 3.6 million babies were born in 1950 (up from 2.8 million at the end of the war five years earlier).[1] And to house this increased demand, we built almost 1.5 million new houses, most of them in the new suburban developments springing up on the outskirts of towns.

The average family income was $3,300 a year.[1] Unemployment was 4.3% and falling, with GDP growth at 8.7%.[2]

Average costs in 1950 [3]	
New house	$8,450
New car	$1,510
Television	$250
Clock Radio	$60
A gallon of gasoline	$0.27

Artist's impression of a family outing in 1950 America.

The family was everything. Fathers commuted to earn a salary. Wives were encouraged to quit their jobs and stay at home. Children walked to school and played outdoors in their well manicured gardens.

Families dined together, watched television together, and enjoyed leisure time and outings together.

[1] U.S. Census Bureau *Estimates of the Population of the United States*: 1950-1954, page 2
[2] thebalance.com/unemployment-rate-by-year-3305506.
[3] thepeoplehistory.com/1950.html.

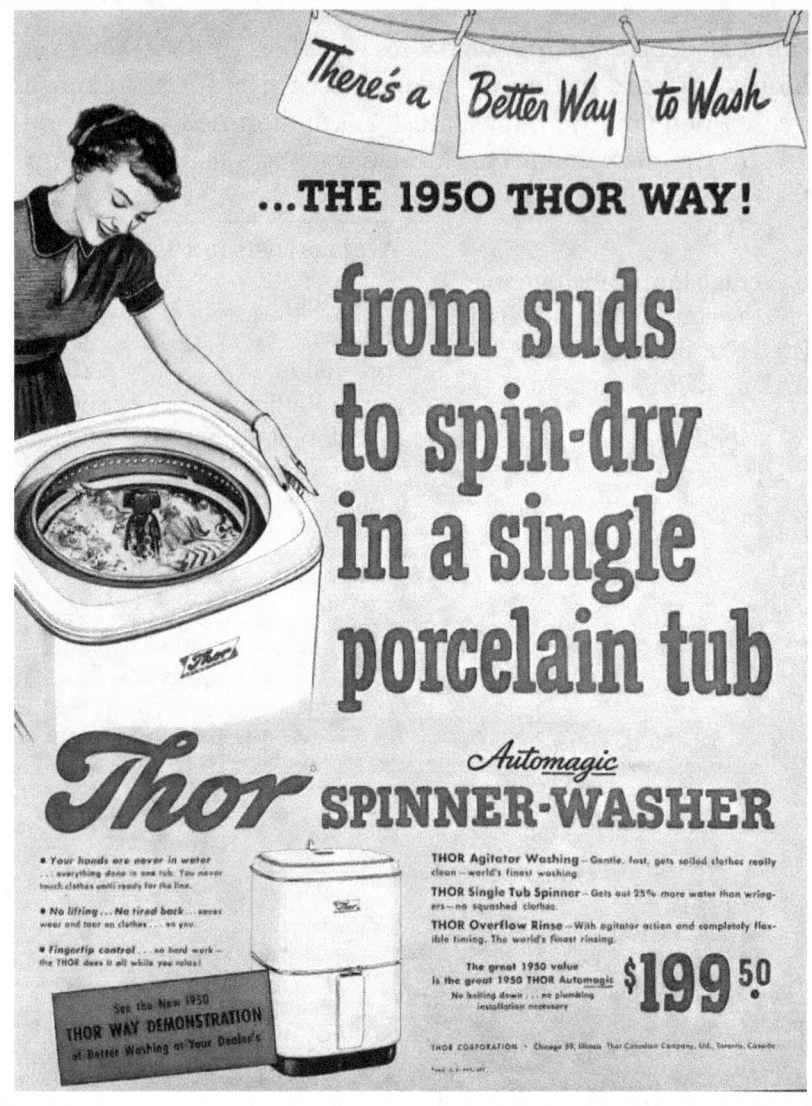

There's a Better Way to Wash...the 1950 Thor Way! from suds to spin-dry in a single porcelain tub   Thor Automatic Spinner-Washer

- Your hands are never in water... everything done in one tub. You never touch clothes until ready for the line. • No lifting... No tired back... saves wear and tear on clothes... on you. • Fingertip control... no hard work–the THOR does it all while you relax!
- THOR Agitator Washing–Gentle, fast, gets soiled clothes really clean–world's finest washing. • THOR Single Tub Spinner–Gets out 25% more water than wringers–no squashed clothes. • THOR Overflow Rinse–With agitator action and completely flexible timing. The world's finest rinsing.

The great 1950 value is the great 1950 THOR Automagic. $199.50
No bolting down... no plumbing installation necessary.
See the New 1950 Thor Way Demonstration of Better Washing at your Dealer's.

Joining the television in our families' list of must-haves were: defrost refrigerators, fully-automatic washing machines, front-loading dryers, vacuum cleaners, air-conditioning and heating units, milkshake makers, and a multitude of other kitchen gadgets and home appliances. In addition we needed a family car or two, bicycles, motorcycles, hiking/ camping/ picnic gear and much, much more.

An energetic and persuasive advertising industry, through TV, radio and print, ensured we always knew what our next purchase needed to be.

"At Last! I'm Free . . .
thanks to my new
WESTINGHOUSE **FROST·FREE*** REFRIGERATOR"

But beneath the appearance of abundance and domestic bliss, Americans were deeply concerned. The Soviets had detonated an atomic bomb in 1949, setting in motion a nuclear race between the two superpowers–the Cold War.

By 1950 both powers were striving to build an even more powerful weapon–the hydrogen bomb.

We would endure another 40 years of tension between the two super-powers before the Cold War finally ended with the dissolution of the Soviet Union in 1991.

A safety education magazine cover from the '50s.

Advertisement

"Perfect Day!"

Typing all day is easy and effortless when you have an IBM Electric. All you do is "touch" the keys–the typewriter does the work. At five o'clock you'll still feel fresh and free from fatigue.

You'll like all the energy-saving features of the IBM Electric, its simple operation, its perfect impressions, its modern styling. You'll like having the world's finest typewriter for your own.

    IBM Electric Typewriters   International Business Machines Corporation

Austerity in the United Kingdom

Now just imagine you flashed back to a town in 1950 United Kingdom or Western Europe.

Unlike boom-time America, a very different, more restrained lifestyle would await you.

London, like many other major European cities, bore the brunt of destruction from the WWII bombings. The rebuilding process was painfully slow, hampered by a general shortage of manpower and construction materials.

A London street scene in 1950.

London, like many other major European cities, bore the brunt of All around the country there was a desperate shortage of housing to accommodate the growing population. Nearly half of those living in the larger cities housed in private, rented, often substandard apartments. While in the country, homes often lacked water, sanitation, electricity and phones.

Stifling and miserable austerity measures had been in place for the preceding ten years. On the 26th May 1950, the UK finally ended petrol rationing. However rationing of meat and other basic foods would stay in place for another four years.

The post-war baby boom, along with a shortage of funds and building materials for new schools, often resulted in crowded classes of up to 50 students in urban areas. Only 30% of 15-year-olds, 14% of 16-year-olds and 7% of 17-year-olds remained in full time education.[1]

Children at school in England in 1950.

Elections held in February 1950 saw an unprecedented 84% voter turnout, returning the Labour Party to power with the help of the powerful trade unions.

Across the United Kingdom, taxes were high with around 6.6% of GDP spent on defence. Average salaries were around £100.[2]

[1] researchbriefings.files.parliament.uk/documents/SN04252/SN04252.pdf.
[2] historytoday.com/archive/britain-1950.

Advertisement

Beautiful new things were done to these 1950 Chryslers

Now on display... the most dramatically new car of the year! Deliberately and excitingly re-styled as no other car! Its beauty outside and inside is new, new, new!... The modern classic! See it... drive it... and compare it! And you'll learn the important difference in Chrysler's kind of beauty. For here–as nowhere else–is beauty that truly reflects the sound engineering and solid comfort and safety inside. The extra headroom, legroom, shoulder-room! The chair-height seats! The full vision all around! All the qualities that have meant so much to you have been retained! Go see your Chrysler dealer today. There's no other car like the all-new Chrysler for 1950!

Beautiful 1950 Chrysler Today's new style classic

Our Love Affair with Automobiles

In just five years since war's end, the US car industry had shifted from fabricating utilitarian war tanks and trucks, to producing fashionable consumer vehicles, the kind of which we just had to have. More than 80% of cars globally were produced in the USA, a figure that has been in decline ever since, as other countries advanced their car industries.

There were now 40.2 million registered cars on US roads, up from 25.7 million five years earlier.[1] Our love affair with cars had begun.

Cars on a Philadelphia traffic circle, 1950.

Detroit had long been the car manufacturing hub of the country, and America led the world in car production, turning out 8 million vehicles in 1950 alone. This equated to around 80% of all new vehicles worldwide.[2]

With the population peaking in 1950 at 1.85 million people, Detroit had become the 4th largest city in the USA.[3] And by the end of the decade, a whopping one in six adults nation-wide would be employed in the car industry.

---

[1] fhwa.dot.gov/ohim/summary95/mv200.pdf.
[2] en.wikipedia.org/wiki/List_of_countries_by_motor_vehicle_production.
[3] theweek.com/articles/461968/rise-fall-detroit-timeline.

Our love affair with cars grew hand-in-hand with the post-war baby boom and housing construction boom. Where would we be without our cars? How else could we get from our far-flung suburban homes to our inner city offices?

Rising incomes saw car ownership soar in the year 1950. An additional 2.4 million vehicles were put on the US roads as families fled the cities for the quiet life of the suburbs.

MERCURY sport sedan—These smooth, slick lines make the six-passenger 1950 Mercury Sport Sedan a car to be admired at first sight. And your first drive will make you admire its down-to-earth roadability. Long, broad, sturdy... the "better than ever" 1950 Mercury Sport Sedan is sure to be a hit with style-wise people wherever it's seen.

Cars were no longer just a necessity; they had become an expression of our personality. Sturdy, sporty, or luxurious, cars now came in a wide range of styles, colors, and price points, with chrome, wings, stripes and fins for added personality.

Advertisement

"Test Drive" a '50 Ford! See, Hear and Feel the Difference

Before you buy any car, your Ford Dealer invites you to "Test Drive" the '50 Ford! "Test Drive" it for power... for comfort... for ease of handling. As for economy–the rapidly growing family of '50 Ford owners has found that this car is designed for top value in original purchase price, and top economy of operation and maintenance. And for looks–well Ford has won the Fashion Academy's Gold Medal again for 1950! See it–"Test Drive" it at your Ford Dealer's today!

• It shines on dress parade... It proves its mettle in action! • It's got 'let's go' starts and 'cat's paw' stops! • It takes the medal for Beauty and it's built to live outdoors!

There's a Ford in your future, with a future built in!

Advertisement

the Wilshire – *with 16" Picture Tube* $499⁹⁵

WITH "TRIPLE-PLAY" PHONOGRAPH! FM-AM DYNAMAGIC RADIO! SUPER-POWERED TV CHASSIS! BUILT-IN ROTO-SCOPE ANTENNA!

Now!... *complete home entertainment* in a magnificent hand-rubbed 18th Century walnut console by one of the world's leading stylists. Engineered to outperform any set, anywhere, any time! Enjoy TV pictures clear as the movies on a huge 16" tube (almost 150 square inches)... so clear you can sit as near to the screen as you please. Easy to tune as a radio. Built-in Roto-Scope antenna assures most powerful station pick-up of all... because *it's directional!* Versatile "Triple-Play" phonograph plays all records (33¼, 45, 78 rpm), all sizes, all automatically with one tone arm, one needle, one spindle. Static-free Dynamagic FM-AM radio... ultra-compact! Generous record storage space. See your nearby Admiral dealer now!

Admiral   America's Smart Set in television

With "triple-play" phonograph! FM-AM dynamagic radio!
Super-powered TV chassis! Built-in roto-scope antenna!

Now!... *Complete home entertainment* in a magnificent hand-rubbed 18th Century walnut console by one of the world's leading stylists. Engineered to outperform any set, anywhere, any time! Enjoy TV pictures clear as the movies on a huge 16" tube (almost 150 square inches)... so clear you can sit as near to the screen as you please. Easy to tune as a radio. Built-in Roto-Scope antenna assures most powerful station pick-up of all... because *it's directional!* Versatile "Triple-Play" phonograph plays all records ($33^1/_2$, 45, 78 rpm), all sizes, all automatically with one tone arm, one needle, one spindle. Static-free Dynamagic FM-AM radio... ultra-compact! Generous record storage space. See your nearby Admiral dealer now!

The Golden Age of Television

By 1950, an estimated 3.8 million American households, equivalent to 9% of the population, owned a television set.[1] And that number would increase exponentially throughout the decade as television became our number one preferred choice of entertainment.

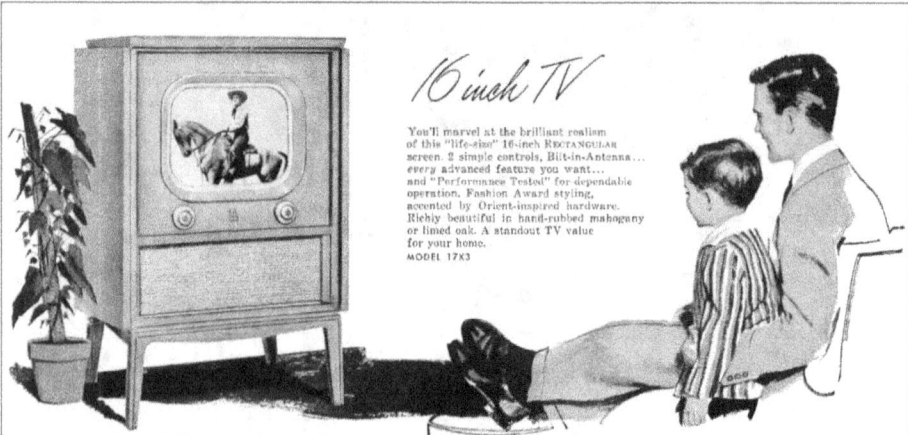

Family focussed Motorola television advertisements from 1950.

For the rising middle classes, television was much more convenient than going to a downtown cinema. It provided an increasing array of programs to watch, it was available every day of the week, and it was free to watch once purchased.

[1] From US Department of Commerce, Bureau of the Census, 1982-83. Page 555. Media Utilization No. 934–1950 to 1982.

Most Popular Television Shows of 1950

1. Texaco Star Theater
2. Fireside Theater
3. Philco TV Playhouse
4. Your Show of Shows
5. The Colgate Comedy Hour
6. Gillette Cavalcade of Sports
7. The Lone Ranger
8. Arthur Godfrey's Talent Scouts
9. Hopalong Cassidy
10. Mama
11. Robert Montgomery Presents
12. Martin Kane, Private Eye
13. Man Against Crime
14. Kraft Television Theatre
15. The Toast of the Town
16. The Aldrich Family
17. You Bet Your Life
18. Arthur Godfrey and His Friends
19. Armstrong Circle Theatre
= Lights Out
= Big Town

* From the Nielsen Media Research 1950-'51 season of top-rated primetime TV series in the USA.

In the early '50s, television continued to rely on live broadcasts of popular radio programs. These programs were much cheaper and faster to produce than made-for-TV dramas.

Comedy-Varieties remained our most popular form of family-time TV entertainment, accounting for six of the top eight programs for the year.

Ed Sullivan, host of *The Toast of the Town* (CBS. 1948-1965).

Also keeping us glued to our screens were highly rated drama series such as *The Lone Ranger, Fireside Theater, Hopalong Cassidy,* and *Martin Kane, Private Eye.*

Clayton Moore and Jay Silverheels in *The Lone Ranger* (ABC. 1949-1957).

Advertisement

The Secret of TV's Brightest Picture Tube!

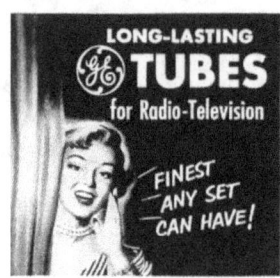

LONG-LASTING GE TUBES for Radio-Television

FINEST ANY SET CAN HAVE!

Do you remember when television viewing was strictly a darkroom pastime... shades down... no lights... eyes straining to follow a dim, foggy picture? How different today, thanks largely to the brighter picture tube developed and made available to the industry by General Electric. Hailed everywhere, this great improvement employs light formerly wasted, to produce brighter, clearer, sharper pictures. The secret: a microscopic aluminized "mirror" superimposed on the picture screen to direct light toward the viewer.

This basic contribution to picture enjoyment is typical of the research that helps make G-E tubes for television and radio as fine as any set can have. For long life and superb performance, specify G-E tubes. Installed by dependable servicemen everywhere.

General Electric Company, Tube Division, Schenectady 5, New York

You can put your confidence in—

GENERAL ⓖⒺ ELECTRIC

The Secret of TV's Brightest Picture Tube!

Do you remember when television viewing was strictly a darkroom pastime...shades down...no lights...eyes straining to follow a dim, foggy picture? How different today, thanks largely to the brighter picture tube developed and made available to the industry by General Electric. Hailed everywhere, this great improvement employs light formerly wasted, to produce brighter, clearer, sharper pictures. The secret: a microscopic aluminized "mirror" superimposed on the picture screen to direct light toward the viewer.

This basic contribution to picture enjoyment is typical of the research that helps make G-E tubes for television and radio as fine as any set can have. For long life and superb performance, specify G-E tubes. Installed by dependable servicemen everywhere.

Long-Lasting GE Tubes for Radio-Television   Finest any set can have!

You can put your confidence in General Electric

Poster for *The Bob Hope Show* (NBC. 1950-1996, various specials).

Ralph Byrd in *Dick Tracy* (ABC. 1950-1951).

The television networks were quick to turn out new programs to keep us tuning in. Here are just a few of the new programs that aired for the first time in 1950: *The Bob Hope Show, Dick Tracy, What's My Line, The Jack Benny Program* and *You Bet Your Life* (host Groucho Marx).

George Fenneman and Groucho Marx in *You Bet Your Life* (NBC-TV. 1950-1961).

The Jack Benny Program (CBS. 1950-1965).

Peanuts Daily Comic Strip Debut

2nd October 1950

Charles Monroe Schulz sketching Charlie Brown in 1956.

Charlie Brown in his first comic strip, 1950.

Charles M. Schultz introduced us to his Peanuts Gang on 2nd October 1950, when seven American newspapers printed his daily comic strip. Schultz was 27 years old at the time. He would go on to create another 50 years of adventures for Charlie Brown and the Gang before his retirement in 1999.

Five decades of Charlie Brown.

A 1950s comic strip showing the early version of Charlie Brown. The black t-shirt zigzag was introduced later that year.

Snoopy first appeared in a Peanuts comic strip in October 1950.

By the time of Schultz's passing in 2000, the Peanuts comic strip was syndicated in over 2,600 newspapers worldwide. The Peanuts Gang continues to inspire and enthral readers to this day, having spawned books, television shows and movies in over 25 languages.[1]

Charlie Brown, Snoopy, Linus, Lucy, Peppermint Patty, and their friends live on in the child within all of us.

[1] Details and figures from Schulzmuseum.org.

Advertisement

Best Ride Money can Buy—*

Costs a Lot Less Money—**

when you go GREYHOUND!

* **Best Ride?** There's a bold claim—but we sincerely believe that Greyhound gives you more relaxation (in body-contoured easy-chairs), more mental ease (behind highly-skilled drivers), and greater scenic enjoyment than any other transportation in the Land!

** **Costs Less?** The easiest way to convince yourself is by calling the nearest Greyhound station—and comparing the fares with those of any other type of travel, public or private. See how you save up to a third or half of every dollar —often more—by Greyhound!

A LOT MORE TRAVEL
for A LOT LESS MONEY

Best Ride Money Can Buy–Costs a Lot Less Money–When you go Greyhound!

Best Ride? There's a bold claim–but we sincerely believe that Greyhound gives you more relaxation (in body-contoured easy chairs), more mental ease (behind highly-skilled drivers), and greater scenic enjoyment than any other transportation in the Land!

Costs Less? The easiest way to convince yourself is by calling the nearest Greyhound station–and comparing the fares with those of any other type of travel. See how you save up to a third or half of every dollar–often more–by Greyhound!

A Lot More Travel for a Lot Less Money!

World's First Credit Card

8th February 1950

On 8th February 1950, Diners' Club became the first credit card to be used when its founder, Frank McNamara, paid for his dinner using a cardboard charge card and his signature.

Diners' club launched with 200 of the founder's friends as members, and 27 participating restaurants. It was marketed as an independent payment card for diners and travelers, allowing patrons to settle their bill at the end of each month through their credit account. Diners would pay $5 per year for the privilege, whilst participating establishments would be charged 7%.

An original Diners Club card from 1950.

By the end of the year Diners' Club would boast 20,000 members, reaching one billion by the time of its listing on the New York Stock Exchange in 1959.

Diners' Club also boasts the privilege of being the first charge card in Russia (1969) and in China (1980).

In 1952, Frank McNamara sold his share of Diners' Club to his partners for a mere $200,000.

Soviet Propaganda Posters

Advertisements

Soviet military propaganda poster, 1950.

Bulgarian Sino-Soviet propaganda poster, 1950.

Sino-Soviet friendship propaganda poster, 1950.

Russian Sino-Soviet propaganda poster, 1950.

The Cold War–Nuclear Arms Race

Cold War tensions between the two former allies–the USSR and the USA–had been increasing since the end of the war in 1945. Starting in the USA as policies for communist containment, the distrust and misunderstanding between the two sides quickly escalated from political squabbling, to a military nuclear arms race. For more than 40 years, the Nuclear Arms Race gave the two superpowers the pretext needed to test nuclear bombs on a massive scale.

After the first atomic (fission) bombs dropped on Hiroshima and Nagasaki in 1945, the US continued testing nuclear bombs on land, sea and air. The Soviets tested their first atomic bomb in August 1949. The Nuclear Arms Race was underway.

On 31st Jan 1950, President Truman gave the green light to develop the much more powerful thermonuclear hydrogen (fusion) bomb.

Ivy Mike, the world's first thermonuclear bomb, was detonated in 1952. The radioactive mushroom cloud from the 10.4 megaton bomb rose 41 km (25.5 mi), with a radius of 161 km (100 mi).

Ivy Mike atmospheric nuclear test, 1st Nov 1952.

By 1950, the US had amassed a stockpile of 299 nuclear weapons. The Soviets were just ramping up, with 5 nuclear weapons at the start of the decade, increasing to 1,605 within the next ten years.

Both sides continued to increase their nuclear stockpiles. The US peaked in 1967 with a total of 31,225 weapons, against the Soviet's 8,339 weapons.[1] The USSR continued to grow their stockpile until 1988 (amassing 23,205 weapons). In 1991, the Nuclear Arms Race ended with the signing of a denuclearization treaty.

Over the years, more than 2,000 nuclear bombs have been tested, with millions of people unwittingly exposed to radioactive fallout.

[1] tandfonline.com/doi/pdf/10.2968/066004008.

North Korea Invades South Korea   25th June 1950

Following numerous clashes along the border between North and South Korea, the North Korean military forces (KPA) advanced into South Korea on 25th June 1950, marking the start of the three-year-long Korean War.

The northern socialist state, financially supported by China and the Soviet Union, sought to reunify the two Koreas under communist rule.

Newspaper headlines from the 26th June 1950.

Fearing a communist global expansion, a United Nations combined force from twenty-one countries pledged to assist the ill prepared South Korean Army. Almost 90% of the military ground personnel sent during the next three years would come from the United States.

The initial months of war saw heavy Allied losses and multiple defeats to the stronger and better equipped KPA ground troops. However, by September, the Allied and South Korean forces broke through into North Korea, pushing the KPA troops towards the border with China.

Crew of an M24 tank along the Naktong River front, 24th Aug 1950.

Grief stricken infantryman whose buddy was killed in action, Haktong-ni area, 28th Aug 1950.

Chinese tanks on parade, Beijing 1950.

On 19th October 1950, in a surprise counterattack, the Chinese Peoples Volunteer Army sent armed forces to battle alongside the KPA.

In response, the USA increased its military involvement, sending more troops to the battle front.

The Korean war ended in July 1953 with the creation of the Korean Demilitarized Zone separating the North and South Koreas. To date no peace treaty has been signed, leaving the two Koreas technically still at war.

3rd Battalion of the Royal Australian Regiment, in Korea.

Canadian Special Forces in Korea, 13th October 1950.

British units en-route to Korea, 25th August 1950.

Advertisement

Officers and Airmen Work Together on the World's Greatest Team!
Whatever position you qualify for on this team, there's a career for you in the US Air Force

Whether your educational background and natural aptitudes fit you for flight training, or for special skilled technical work in any of the challenging new career fields that are open to you in today's Air Force, you owe it to yourself to investigate your opportunities. As Officer or Airman, as pilot, navigator, air crew member, or ground crew technician–when you're in the Air Force you're on a team whose watchword is success. Get full details on the Aviation Cadet, Officer Candidate, and Airmen Career programs at your nearest U.S. Air Force Base or Recruiting Station today. Get on the team!

• College Trained Men...If you are single, between the ages of 20 and 26½, with at least two years of college and have high physical and moral qualifications, you may be accepted for Aviation Cadet training as either Pilot or Navigator. Upon completion of one year of training you receive a reserve commission as an officer in the U.S. Air Force, and begin a three year tour of active duty.

• Men With High School Training...If you are between the ages of 17 and 34, single, with high physical and moral qualifications, you may be accepted for special technical training in aviation, radar, electronics, or any one of 42 Airmen Career fields. The Air Force today offers every Airman full opportunity for steady advancement in a rewarding lifetime career.

South African Apartheid Laws 27th April 1950

On 27th April 1950, the white minority government of South Africa passed into law the *Group Areas Act*, formally segregating the different races based on skin color. Ownership and occupation of land would be restricted to specific racial groups within specific areas. The law strengthened the existing Apartheid policies, allowing for forcible, and often violent, removal of non-whites from white designated areas.

Protest marches and police action in South Africa, 1950.

Around the same time, several other supporting Acts of Parliament were created, each designed to cement in place the Apartheid system. These included *the Population Registration Act* of 1950, (to classify every South African according to race) and *the Immorality Act* of 1950, (to prohibit interracial marriage or sex). *The Suppression of Communism Act* of 1950 was a broadly defined act which included any opposition to government, further allowing for the suppression of the black majority.

The Acts were strengthened and amended multiple times over subsequent years.

Following decades of international condemnation and sanctions, the laws were finally repealed in 1991 with the dismantling of the Apartheid system.

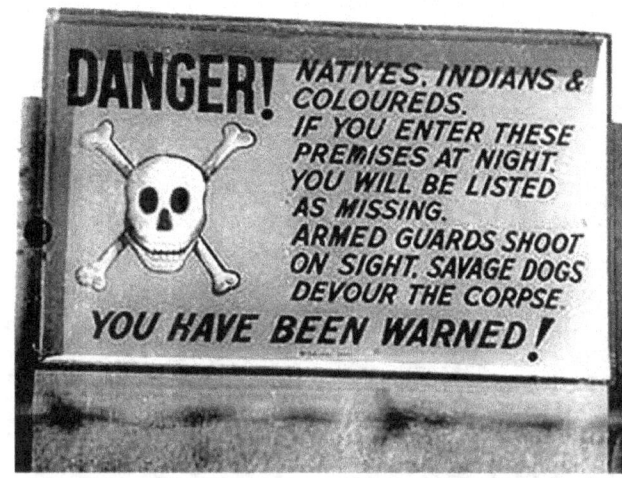

Area warning signs were commonplace.

India–A Country is Born

26th January 1950

On 26th January 1950, a new constitution was signed giving birth to the Republic of India. The new democratic country was to be organized as a federal union of territories and states, ruled under a parliamentary system.

Commemorative stamp, India 1950.

Dr. Rajendra Prasad, India's first president, at the Republic Day celebration on 26th January 1950.

The transition away from British rule was by no means a peaceful one. During the bloody partition years that followed, it is estimated that more than one million people died and 10 million were forced to relocate. The separation of the Muslim north from India resulted in the creation of the Dominion of Pakistan.

The Great Brink's Robbery

17th January 1950

On 17th January 1950, a gang of eleven armed robbers pulled off a heist that was to become the "crime of the century". $1.2 million in cash and $1.6 million in checks and securities were stolen from the Brinks Building in Boston, MA. At the time, it was the largest robbery in the history of the USA.

An news reporter wears a rubber mask similar to that worn by seven of the bandits. He points to a name plate on first of six locked doors opened by the gunmen.

Masterminded by Joseph "Big Joe" McGinnis, the attack had been skillfully planned for more than a year. The gang had trained, rehearsed, and fabricated costumes. They also created exact copies of keys, lock cylinders and building plans. They were well prepared. Police found very little evidence at the crime scene and spent the next six years chasing dead-end leads.

On 6th January 1956, police apprehended one of the gang on an unrelated charge. He confessed to the crime. During the following weeks, just days before the statute of limitations was up, the surviving gang members were arrested. Only $58,000 of the stolen money was ever recovered.

The heist has inspired a number of books, movies and television adaptations.

The eleven Brinks robbers, 1956.

The snowman never melts in snapshots

Around home, so much happens that you don't want to forget. Fun in the snow. A new puppy or kitten. They all come back "like yesterday" when you take pictures.

With your camera ready, and two or three extra rolls of Kodak Film on hand, it's so easy to keep your snapshot record up to date. And you can give your family and friends a great treat–"the latest news"–with extra prints... Remember, the snapshots you'll want tomorrow, you must take today.

Eastman Kodak Company, Rochester 4, N. Y.

Only Eastman makes Kodak Cameras and Kodak Film

Kodak Duallex Camera makes wonderful snapshots–easily. Negative, $2^{1}/4 \times 2^{1}/4$. With Kodak Lens, $12.75, with Kodak f/8 Lens, $19.85. Flasholder, $3.33. Prices include Federal Tax.

Vintage Airline Posters from 1950.

Marlon Brando Silver Screen Debut

20th July 1950

Born 3rd April 1924, Marlon Brando ranks as one of the greatest actors of all time. Following a brief six years on Broadway, he made his film debut in Fred Zimmermann's haunting drama *The Men* in 1950, and quickly become one of cinema's most sought after and highly paid actors.

Marlon Brando in *The Men* (United Artists, 1950).

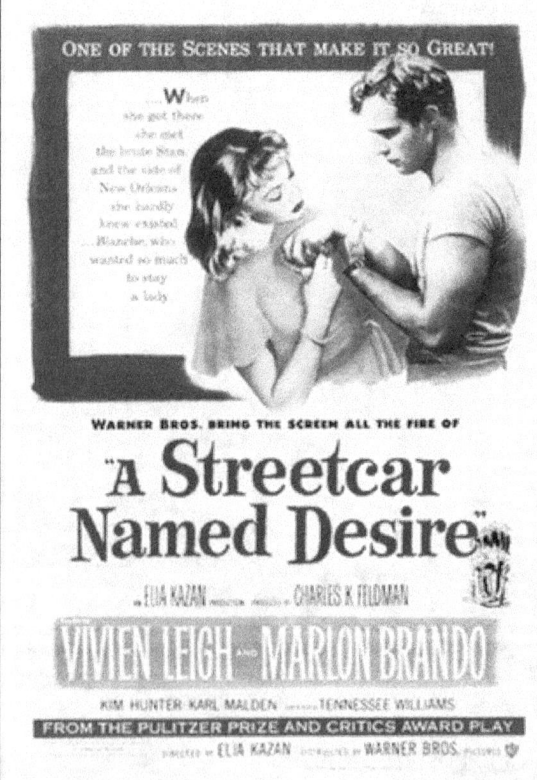

A Streetcar Named Desire poster (Warner Bros. 1951).

In 1951, Brando received his first Oscar nomination for his performance in *A Streetcar Named Desire*. He would go on to win two Oscars, four Golden Globes and three BAFTAs, among countless other nominations and acting awards.

In 1962 he became the first male actor to earn more than $1 million for a single film, when he was signed for *Mutiny on the Bounty*.

With his brooding good looks, sex symbol status, and a career spanning 60 years, Brando is most noted for his performances in:
Julius Caesar (1953),
On the Waterfront (1954),
The Wild One (1957),
The Godfather (1972),
Last Tango in Paris (1972)
and *Apocalypse Now* (1979).

As Marc Anthony in *Julius Caesar* (MGM. 1953).

With Mary Murphy in *The Wild One* (Colombia Pictures, 1953).

With Eva Marie Saint in *On the Waterfront* (Colombia Pictures, 1954).

As Vito Corleone in *The Godfather* (Paramount Pictures, 1972).

1950 in Cinema and Film

Highest Paid Stars
1. John Wayne
2. Bob Hope
3. Bing Crosby
4. Betty Grable
5. James Stewart

Bob Hope with Lucille Ball in *Fancy Pants* (1950, Paramount Pictures).

Cinema attendance reached its peak in the mid-1940s and faced a steady decline throughout the 1950s. With more and more families filling their leisure time with the convenience of television, the motion-picture industry needed to find new ways to win over new audiences.

Younger audiences now had cash to spare. Movies themes adjusted to accommodate the new trends in popular culture, and to exploit the sex appeal of young, rising stars such as Marilyn Monroe, James Dean and Marlon Brando.

Marilyn Monroe in 1953.

John Wayne in *Rio Grande* (Republic Pictures, 1950).

1950 film debuts

Marlon Brando	The Men
Tippi Hedren	The Petty Girl
Sophia Loren	Totò Tarzan
Rita Moreno	So Young, So Bad
Peter Sellers	The Black Rose
Jack Palance	Panic in the Streets
Robert Wagner	The Happy Years

* From en.wikipedia.org/wiki/1950_in_film.

Top Grossing Films of the Year

1	King Solomon's Mines	MGM	$9,955,000
2	All About Eve	20th Century Fox	$8,400,000
3	Cinderella	Disney	$8,000,000
4	Annie Get Your Gun	MGM	$7,756,000
5	Father of the Bride	MGM	$6,084,000
6	Sunset Boulevard	Paramount	$5,000,000
7	Born Yesterday	Columbia	$4,150,000
8	Wabash Avenue	20th Century Fox	$4,054,000
9	At War with the Army	Paramount	$3,100,000
10	My Blue Heaven	20th Century Fox	$3,000,000

* From en.wikipedia.org/wiki/1950_in_film by box office gross in the USA.

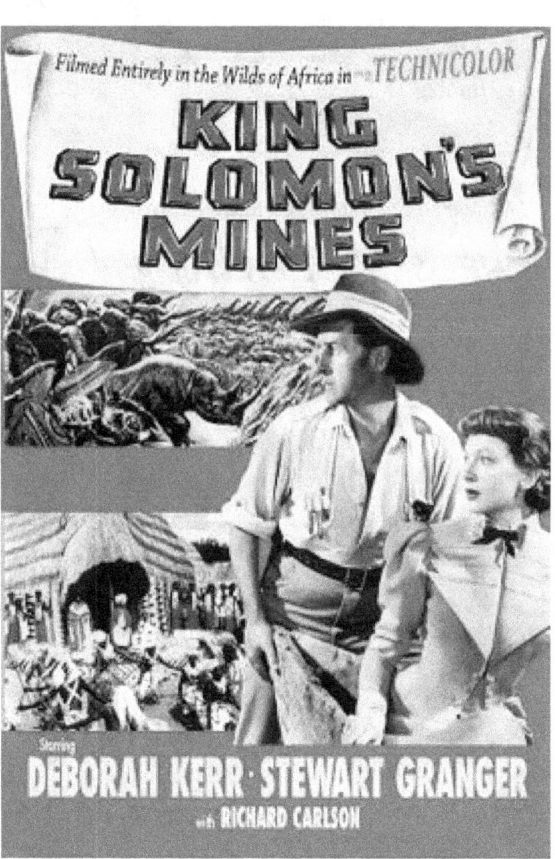

1950 Cold War Inspired Films

Spy Hunt by Universal Pictures.

Guilty of Treason by Freedom Productions.

I Married a Communist by RKO Pictures.

Destination Moon by George Pal Productions.

Advertisement

The candy bar that's like a chocolate nut sundae!
Chocolate. First bite, chocolate...
pure Mars milk chocolate, poured on thick as it'll stay!
Almonds. Then crispy, whole almonds, the expensive kind,
toasted till they're gold. Plenty of them!
Nougat. Rich, creamy nougat that comes from fresh egg whites
and pure sugar whipped till it's fluffy!

The boys at Mars say: "You ought to see how we put this together!"

We stir it up in the sunniest kitchens you ever saw. Sweet milk chocolate, sugar white as snow, selected meaty almonds. With strictly fresh eggs and pure, Grade A milk straight from "down on the farm"!

Guys and Dolls Hits Broadway

24th November 1950

Broadway classic *Guys and Dolls* premiered on 24th November 1950, at the 46th Street Theater in New York City. It was an instant smash hit. New York critics celebrated this "perfect musical comedy", which went on for a 1200-performance run.

The musical won five Tony awards in 1951. It opened in London in 1953 and has since seen several Broadway and international revivals.

Theatrical poster from 1950.

Robert Alda and Isabel Bigley on the set of *Guys and Dolls*.

Guys and Dolls film poster (MGM. 1955).

In 1955, a movie version was released. It starred Marlon Brando and Frank Sinatra, two of Hollywood's biggest names, in the leading male roles.

The Lion, the Witch and the Wardrobe   16th Oct 1950

Between 1950 and 1956, children's author C. S. Lewis published *The Chronicles of Narnia*, a series of seven fantasy novels set in the mythical land of Narnia. *The Lion, the Witch and the Wardrobe* was the first of the series and the best known of the seven books. The book was instantly popular with young readers.

Released on 16th October 1950, publisher Geffrey Bles feared the book would not sell well. At the time children's books were realistic in nature. Fantasy books were considered inappropriate and potentially harmful to children.

Original cover for the first edition of
The Lion, the Witch and the Wardrobe.

Film posters for the three Disney movies.

The book has since been published in nearly 50 languages, remaining popular till this day. It has been adapted for theater, television and film. Since 2005, Disney has released the films of the first three books in the series: *The Lion, the Witch and the Wardrobe, Prince Caspian* and *The Voyage of the Dawn Treader*.

Advertisement

Zenith Announces the Simplest All-Speed Automatic Record Changer Ever Invented!

NEW ZENITH "COBRA-MATIC" VARIABLE SPEED RECORD CHANGER

First and only changer that plays any speed record now made or yet to come, 10 R.P.M. to 85 . . . with two simple controls a six-year-old can operate.

Record lovers—here is the changer that sets you free *forever* from the nightmare of speeds, sizes, attachments and adjustments!

Zenith engineers, who revolutionized record reproduction with the world-famous Cobra® Tone Arm, have now brought you an automatic changer—the new "Cobra-Matic"—so unbelievably simple that you simply won't believe it until you operate it yourself!

You touch one control knob—and set it for any size record—7, 10 or 12 inch! You touch the other control knob—and set it for any speed! Yes, for 33⅓, 45, 78, or any speed from 10 R.P.M. to 85 that the modern world may dream up! You can play them all—with one marvelous new Super-Cobra Tone Arm—not even a needle to adjust, not even one single attachment to fuss with!

And what a glorious outpouring of tone will greet your ears! Zenith's new Super-Cobra, resting a mere ⅕ of an ounce on the record, brings out new tonal beauty against a background of velvety quiet. Reproduces music on a Radionic wave like no other method you have ever seen or heard!

Now—at last—you can buy a phonograph without fear that it will be obsolete. You can be sure that in a Zenith you possess the last word in tonal magnificence and the simplest way ever devised for automatic record playing. See your Zenith dealer today, and see for yourself!

New "Cobra-Matic" Changer Now on All Zenith Radio-Phonographs and Television Combinations

New Zenith "Cobra-Matic" Variable Speed Record Changer

First and only changer that plays any speed record now made or yet to come, 10 R.P.M. to 85...with two simple controls a six-year-old can operate.

Record lovers—here is the changer that sets you free *forever* from the nightmare of speeds, sizes, attachments and adjustments!

Zenith engineers, who revolutionized record reproduction with the world-famous Cobra Tone Arm, have now brought you an automatic changer—the new Cobra-Matic—so unbelievably simple that you simply won't believe it until you operate it yourself!

You touch one control knob—and set it for any size record—7, 10 or 12 inch! You touch the other control knob—and set it for any speed! Yes, for 33¹/3, 45, 78, or any speed from 10R.P.M. to 85 that the modern world may dream up! You can play them all—with one marvelous new Super Cobra Tone Arm—not even a needle to adjust, not even one single attachment to fuss with! And what a glorious outpouring of tone will greet your ears! Zenith's new Super-Cobra, resting a mere ¹/5 of an ounce on the record, brings out new tonal beauty against a background of velvety quiet. Reproduces music on a Radionic wave like no other method you have ever seen or heard!

Now—at last—you can buy a phonograph without fear that it will be obsolete. You can be sure that in a Zenith you possess the last word in tonal magnificence and the simplest way ever devised for automatic record playing. See your Zenith dealer today!

Musical Memories

Music of the early '50s was smooth and mellow, with lyrics focused on story telling and expressing heartfelt emotion. Classic pop crooners with velvety voices led us to joyous highs and the depths of despair. We had yet to discover the electrifying beats of rock 'n' roll.

Music of the early '50s fell into one of three distinct styles—country, R&B, and pop music. In 1950, there was little cross over between the styles. Radio stations focused on one genre, allowing listeners easy access to their preferred type of music.

After several years rising in the music charts, Patti Page reached #1 in 1950 with multiple singles. Her best selling *Tennessee Waltz* was one of the biggest-selling singles of the 20th century. Page blended music genres, becoming the first (and only) artist to have a #1 record on the Pop, R&B and Country charts concurrently.

Nat King Cole began his solo career in 1950, after many years performing as a jazz musician. He achieved immediate success with *Mona Lisa*, becoming one of the great stars of song and screen throughout the 50s and 60s. In 1957, Cole became the first African American to host his own TV show. The Nat 'King' Cole Show aired on NBC for 42 episodes.

1950 Billboard Top 30 Songs

	Artist	Song Title
1	Gordon Jenkins and The Weavers	Goodnight Irene
2	Nat King Cole	Mona Lisa
3	Anton Karas	Third Man Theme
4	Gary and Bing Crosby	Sam's Song
5	Gary and Bing Crosby	Simple Melody
6	Teresa Brewer	Music, Music, Music
7	Guy Lombardo	Third Man Theme
8	Red Foley	Chattanoogie Shoe Shine Boy
9	Sammy Kaye	Harbor Lights
10	Sammy Kaye and Don Cornell	It Isn't Fair

Gordon Jenkins.

Kay Starr.

Sammy Kaye, 1952.

Guy Lombardo, 1944.

	Artist	Song Title
11	Eileen Barton	If I Knew You Were Coming I'd have Baked A Cake
12	Kay Starr	Bonaparte's Retreat
13	Gordon Jenkins and The Weavers	Tzena, Tzena, Tzena
14	Tony Martin	There's No Tomorrow
15	Phil Harris	The Thing
16	Ames Brothers	Sentimental Me
17	Andrews Sisters and Gordon Jenkins	I Wanna Be Loved
18	Patti Page	Tennessee Waltz
19	Andrews Sisters and Gordon Jenkins	I Can Dream, Can't I
20	Tennessee Ernie Ford and Kay Starr	I'll Never Be Free

Perry Como, 1956.

Bing Crosby, 1942.

	Artist	Song Title
21	Patti Page	All My Love
22	Gordon Jenkins	My Foolish Heart
23	Ames Brothers	Rag Mop
24	Bill Snyder	Bewitched
25	Perry Como	Hoop-Dee-Doo
26	Gordon Jenkins	Bewitched
27	Ames Brothers	Can Anyone Explain?
28	Billy Eckstine	My Foolish Heart
29	Bing Crosby	Dear Hearts & Gentle People
30	Frankie Laine	Cry Of The Wild Goose

* From the *Billboard* top 30 singles of 1950.

Advertisement

Magicair Home Hair Dryer

SAVES TIME
SAVES MONEY

Wash and set your hair—then simply relax in your favourite chair—at home. Own a Magicair—and your "appointment only" worries are over. *You* fix the time—*you* name the day—there's no waiting with your own Magicair Hair Dryer.

Magicair is a really professional hair dryer for your home, with a choice of hot or cold drying air. It's well within your budget too.

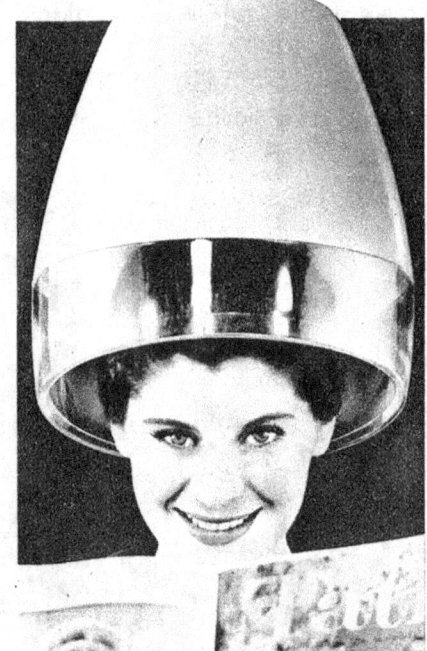

See how simply the Magicair can be fitted to a table or chair back. No more aching arms—just sit back and read your favourite magazine and the Magicair does the work.

8 GUINEAS
(Tax paid. Plus 2s. 7d. P.T. surcharge.)

Obtainable at Electricity Board Showrooms or your local electrical appliance dealer, or write direct to WOMAN & HOME for further information and our free leaflet which shows fabulous hair styles by French of London.

Magicair Hoe Hair Dryer   Saves time saves money

Wash and set your hair–then simply relax in your favourite chair–at home. Own a Magicair–and your "appointment only" worries are over. *You* fix the time–*you* name the day–there's no waiting with your own Magicair Hair Dryer.

Magicair is a really professional hair dryer for your home, with a choice of hot or cold drying air. It's well within your budget too.

See how simply the Magicair can be fitted to a table or chair back. No more aching arms–just sit back and read your favourite magazine and the Magicair does the work.

Fashion Trends of the 1950s

With the misery and bleakness of the war years behind us, the '50s were a time to show off. Consumerism was now a way of life and we were all too willing to spend money on luxuries, non-essentials, and fashion.

How we looked and how we dressed became important everyday considerations for women and men. We spent money like never before, guided by our favorite fashion icons, and helped along by a maturing advertising industry which flooded us with fashion advice through newspapers, magazines, billboards, radio and television.

Clothing manufacturers had perfected mass production techniques while providing military uniforms during the war years. They now shifted their focus to well made, stylish, ready-to-wear clothes.

Mademoiselle magazine cover, June 1950.

The American Weekly cover, April 1950.

The American Magazine cover, April 1950.

Fashion was no longer a luxury reserved for the wealthy. Now the growing middle class could also afford to be fashionable. Magazines and mail-order catalogs kept us informed of the latest trends in fashion, make-up, and accessories.

Advertisement

Dresses from the *National Bellas Hess* mail order catalog in a mix of the "tea skirt" and "sheath" styles that were popular in the early '50s.

Christian Dior's "New Look" from 1947.

As with before the war, all eyes looked to Paris for new directions in haute couture. In 1947 Christian Dior didn't disappoint, unveiling his glamorous, extravagant, ultra-feminine "New Look" to the world.

Gone were the boxy tailored jackets with padded shoulders and slim, short skirts. Paris had brought back femininity, with clinched waists, fuller busts and hips, and longer, wider skirts. The emphasis was on abundance. The New Look set the standard for the entire decade of the 1950s.

The "New Look" in the early '50s.

To achieve this impossible hourglass figure, corsets and girdles were sold in record numbers. Metal underwire bras made a comeback, and a new form of bra known as the "cathedral bra" or "bullet bra" became popular.

Early '50s bullet bra and girdle from Jantzen.

Despite criticisms against the extravagance of the New Look, and arguments that heavy corsets and paddings undermined the freedoms women had won during the war years, the New Look was embraced on both sides of the Atlantic. Before long, inexpensive, ready-to-wear versions of Dior's New Look had found their way into our department store catalogs.

Catalog dresses from Alden's 1954 Spring-Summer Collection.

Dior also created a slimmed down alternative look, as a sleek dress or elegant straight skirt with short jacket. This figure-hugging, groomed and tailored look, known as the sheath dress, continued to place emphasis on the hourglass figure.

Also known as the "wiggle dress", this sexier figure-hugging silhouette was preferred by movie stars such as Marilyn Monroe.

Women embraced the femininity of 1950s fashion from head to toe. Hats, scarves, belts, gloves, shoes, stockings, handbags and jewelry were all given due consideration.

Out on the street, no outfit would be complete without a full complement of matching accessories.

Not much changed in the world of men's fashion during the 1950s. Business attire shifted just a little. Suits were slimmer, and ties were narrower. Skinny belts were worn over pleated pants. Hats, though still worn, were on the way out.

Marlon Brando.

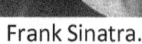

Frank Sinatra.

James Dean.

For the younger generation however, the fashion icons of the day set the trends. James Dean and Marlon Brando made the white T-shirt and blue jeans the must-have items in casual attire. Worn alone, or under an unbuttoned shirt or jacket, the look made working class style a middle-class fashion statement.

Smooth Lip Loveliness that Lasts Cashmere Bouquet Lipstick.
8 fashionable shades that go on, stay on, without smearing.

Smoothly, evenly does it with exciting Cashmere Bouquet Lipstick–never a fear of a rub or smear! So clinging, creamy, caressing, your lips take on a *new* look... an *alive* look... one that says, plain as day, "I *dare* you"! And of course no other lipstick, at any price, betters Cashmere Bouquet's range of fashionable reds. Get Cashmere Bouquet today, and then, *try* to go back to your previous brand. Yes, you're sentenced for life... but you'll love it!

In smart new swivel case. Only 25¢
Look your loveliest with Cashmere Bouquet

Advertisement

Don't Settle for Less!   Feel like a million!
Why accept less when you can be sure of complete comfort with Jockey Underwear! It fits snug as your skin, moves as you move, gives you positive masculine support. Look for the mark, "Y-FRONT," on the garment–it's your assurance that you're getting the famous Coopers product... and one of may reasons why Jockey gives you a real lift. See your dealer soon–be "Hip-Taped" for perfect fit–then feel like a million in Jockey brand Underwear! Jockey Contoured Shirts to match.

Wear Jockey Underwear made only by Coopers.

Comfort for your every need–for every occasion.

• Jockey Shorts for active sport. • Jockey Midway for everyday wear. • Jockey Over-Knee for upper-leg protection. • Jockey Longs for full-leg protection. • Jockey Beilin for dress-up wear.

The famous brand of knit support underwear.
Also Jockey brand Underwear in Children's sizes.

4ᵗʰ British Empire Games   4ᵗʰ–11ᵗʰ January 1950

The idea of a sporting competition among member countries of the British Empire was first proposed in the 19ᵗʰ Century and came to fruition with the 1ˢᵗ British Empire Games held in 1930. The 2ⁿᵈ and 3ʳᵈ Games were held in 1934 and 1938 respectively.

Advertisement commemorating the 1950 Games.

Interrupted by the Second World War, twelve years would pass before the 4ᵗʰ British Empire Games could be held in Christchurch, New Zealand. Twelve Commonwealth countries sent 590 athletes to complete, with an estimated 250,000 people attending.

A film crew capturing an unidentified swimmer competing in the games.

Now known as the Commonwealth Games, 71 nations representing one-third of the global population come together every four years,

> "in the spirit of true sportsmanship ... and ... for the honour of our Commonwealth and for the glory of sport".[1]

[1] Oath of the Commonwealth Games.

First FIA World Championship

13th May 1950

British Grand Prix at Silverstone 1950, Alfa Romeo's Giuseppe Farina leads teammate Luigi Fagioli.

The FIA[1] Formula One (F1) World Championship of Drivers inaugural season commenced in Silverstone, UK, on 13th May 1950. Six Grand Prix races held over four months in Europe, plus the Indianapolis 500, saw fourteen teams participate, along with some privately entered cars. Alfa Romeo dominated throughout with their pre-war supercharged 158. Italian Giuseppe "Nino" Farina won the championship.

[1] Fédération Internationale de l'Automobile.

1950 Poster, Monaco Grand Prix.   Giuseppe "Nino" Farina. Alfa Romeo 158.

"I lived in Milwaukee, I ought to know... Blatz is Milwaukee's finest beer!"

Says Uta Hagen famous star of "Streetcar Named Desire" and many other Broadway hits.

"Wisconsinites like me are used to fine beers," says Uta Hagen. "Because Milwaukee is America's premium beer capital, we always have our choice of the best. And, like most Milwaukeeans, I choose Blatz. It's Milwaukee's *finest* beer!" Yes, *official figures* show that Blatz is the *largest-selling beer in Milwaukee and in all Wisconsin,* too! Try Blatz Beer today!

Uta Hagen's career includes teaching theatre classes, directing experimental productions, playing the piano. She also loves to cook. "My refrigerator is always crowded with good things to eat—and plenty of Blatz Beer, too!" says Uta.

Take a tip from Uta Hagen. Ask for Blatz Beer at your favorite club, tavern, restaurant, or neighborhood store. Remember Blatz is Milwaukee's *finest* beer!

Advertisement

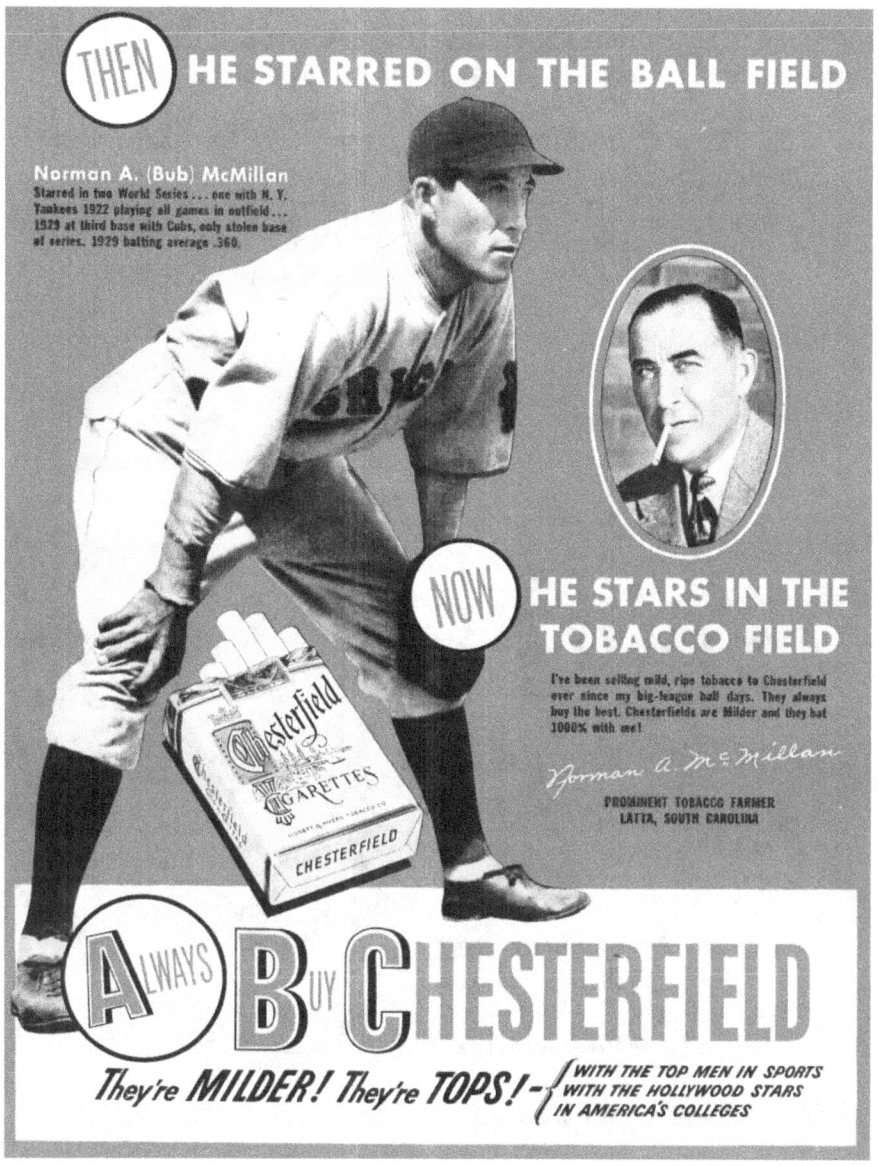

Then–He starred on the ball field.

Norman A. (Bub) McMillan–Starred in two World Series... one with N.Y. Yankees 1922 playing all games in outfield... 1929 at third base with Cubs, only stolen base of series. 1929 batting average 360.

Now–He stars in the tobacco field.

I've been selling mild, ripe tobacco to Chesterfield ever since my big-league ball days. They always buy the best. Chesterfields are Milder and they bat 1000% with me! –Norman A. McMillan. Prominent tobacco farmer, Latta, South Carolina.

Always Buy Chesterfield. They're milder! They're tops!–

With the top men in sports. With the Hollywood stars. In America's colleges.

Other Sporting Events from 1950

30th Jan– Louise Brough beat Doris Hart 6-4, 3-6, 6-4 in an all-American final at the Australian Championships Women's Tennis.

14th Jan– Moroney scored cricket twin centuries for Australia in Johannesburg, South Africa.

25th Mar– Wales outclassed France, 21-0 at Cardiff to clinch the Five Nations Rugby Championship, Grand Slam and Triple Crown.

9th Apr– Jimmy Demaret became the first 3-time Masters champion at the 14th US Masters Tournament, Augusta National GC.

25th Apr– Chuck Cooper became the first African American to be drafted into the NBA (for Boston Celtics).

21st Jun– 2,000th hit for Joe DiMaggio, Yanks beat Indians 8-2.

29th Jun– US beat England 1-0 in a world cup soccer game (next win would not be until 1994).

16th Jul– At the 1950 FIFA World Cup Final in Estádio do Maracanã, Rio de Janeiro: Alcides Ghiggia scored a 79th minute winner as Uruguay beat Brazil, 2-1.

22nd Aug– Althea Gibson became the 1st black competitor in a US national tennis competition.

7th AUG– Tour de France: Ferdinand Kübler became the first Swiss to win the Tour.

26th Aug– Australia beat US (4-1) at the 39th Davis Cup in New York.

29th Aug– The International Olympic Committee voted to admit West Germany and Japan for the next Olympic Games to be held in 1952. Both teams had been banned following WWII.

17th Sep– San Francisco 49ers played their 1st NFL game, losing 21-17.

1st Oct– Babe Zaharias tied Open scoring record (291, par-9) to beat Betsy Rawls by 9 strokes at the US Open Women's Golf, Rolling Hills Country Club, Wichita, Kansas.

31st Oct– The Big Cat, Earl Lloyd became the first African-American to play an NBA game, scoring 6 points for the Washington Capitols.

2nd Dec– South African world bantam weight boxing champion Vic Toweel set a record for knockdowns in a title fight against Englishman Danny Sullivan in Johannesburg. Sullivan floored 14 times in 10 rounds before fighting stopped.

Other News from 1950

31st Jan– Harry S. Truman, President of the USA, ordered the development of a hydrogen (fusion) bomb in direct response to the Soviet detonation of an atomic bomb just four months earlier. Two years later, the US succeeded in creating the more powerful hydrogen bomb, testing it for the first time in the Pacific in 1952. The Soviets tested their first hydrogen bomb in 1953.

8th Feb– The Stasi (Ministry for State Security) was founded in East Germany. Modeled after the Soviet KGB, the Stasi was responsible for both domestic political surveillance and foreign espionage.

12th Feb– Albert Einstein warned of mutual destruction should nuclear war be the eventual outcome of the Cold War.

14th Feb– A mutual defense and assistance treaty was signed by the two communist powers–the Soviet Union and the People's Republic of China–giving the West further argument that communism was a dangerous international movement.

9th May– L. Ron Hubbard published *Dianetics: A Modern Science of Mental Health*. In this book he introduced the self-help concept of Dianetics, which forms the basis of Scientology.

17th Jun– Dr. Richard Lawler performed the world's first successful kidney transplant on patient Ruth Tucker (49) in Illinois USA. The kidney would function for just 53 days, before being removed due to medical complications . Ruth lived a further 5 years.

16th Sep– The Journal of the American Medical Association published two articles outlining a six hundred and eighty-four case study proving the link between cigarette smoking and cancer.

13th Nov– The President of Venezuela, Colonel Carlos Delgado Chalbaud, was kidnapped and murdered in Caracas.

22nd Nov– Shirley Temple announced her retirement from show business at age 22.

13th Dec– James Dean secured his first acting break, playing the part of a fun-loving teenager in a Pepsi Commercial. His good looks and acting talent caught the eye of scouts, who wasted no time launching him to movie star status.

Advertisement

Famous People Born in 1950

5th Jan– Chris Stein, American guitarist & co-founder of Blondie.

20th Jan– Mahamane Ousmane, President of Niger (1993-1996).

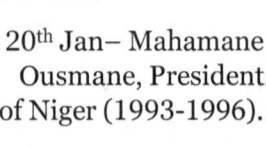

13th Feb– Peter Gabriel, English singer.

18th Feb– Cybill Shepherd, actress.

24th Feb– George Thorogood, American singer & guitarist.

26th Feb– Helen Clark, New Zealand Prime Minister (1999-2008).

27th Feb– Franco Moschino, Italian fashion designer.

2nd Mar– Karen Carpenter, American vocalist & drummer.

4th Mar– Rick Perry, American politician, Governor of Texas (2000-2015).

13th Mar– Bernard Julien, West Indies cricketer.

17th Mar– Betty Dukes, American Walmart employee & discrimination activist.

26th Mar– Alan Silvestri, American film score composer.

30th Mar– Robbie Coltrane, Scottish actor.

5th Apr– Agnetha Fältskog [Anna Ulvaeus], Swedish singer (ABBA).

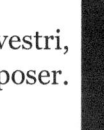
12th Apr– David Cassidy, American singer & actor.

18th Apr– Kenny Ortega, American film & TV producer.

28th Apr– Jay Leno, American comedian & TV talk show host.

13th May– Stevie Wonder, American singer-songwriter.

22nd May– Bernie Taupin, British singer & lyricist.

23rd May– Martin McGuinness, Irish Sinn Féin politician & IRA member.

14th Jun– Rowan Williams, 104th Archbishop of Canterbury, UK.

5th July– Huey Lewis, American musician.

15th July– Arianna Huffington, creator of The Huffington Post.

18th July– Richard Branson, British entrepreneur.

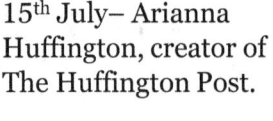

9th Aug– Chris Haney, Canadian journalist & creator of "Trivial Pursuit".

11th Aug– Steve Wozniak, co-founder of Apple Computer.

15th Aug– Anne Elizabeth Alice Louise Windsor, British Princess.

1st Sep– Phil McGraw, American psychologist (Dr. Phil).

12th Sep– Gustav Brunner, Austrian Formula One designer & engineer.

7th Sep– Narendra Modi, 15th Prime Minister of India.

21st Sep– Bill Murray, American actor & comedian.

31st Oct– Zaha Hadid, British architect.

31st Oct– John Candy, Canadian actor and comedian (d.1994).

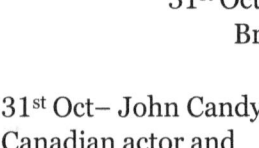
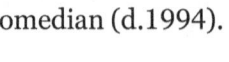

Advertisement

DeLuxe: Specially elegant...uncommon.   Webster

Walker's De Luxe is a straight Bourbon whiskey,
Elegant in taste, uncommonly good–a Hiram Walker whiskey.

Hiram Walker & Sons Inc.

1950 in Numbers

Census Statistics [1]

- Population of the world — 2.5 billion
- Population in the United States — 158.8 million
- Population in the United Kingdom — 50.62 million
- Population in Canada — 13.73 million
- Population in Australia — 8.18 million
- Average age for marriage of women — 20.3 years old
- Average age for marriage of men — 22.8 years old
- Average family income USA — $3,300 per year
- Minimum wage USA — $0.75 per hour

Costs of Goods [2]

- Average home $7,500-$8,500
- Average new car $1,510
- New Cadillac Series 62 $3,650
- A gallon of gasoline $0.27
- A pack of cigarettes $0.15
- A loaf of bread $0.12
- A gallon of milk $0.82
- T bone steak $0.59 per pound
- Lamb chops $0.49 per pound
- Sliced bacon $0.35 per pound
- Potatoes $0.35 for 5 pounds
- Large eggs $0.49 per dozen
- Kraft cheese slices $0.29 per pack.
- Frozen green beans $0.24 per half pound

---

[1] Figures taken from worldometers.info/world-population, US National Center for Health Statistics, Divorce and Divorce Rates US (cdc.gov/nchs/data/series/sr_21/sr21_029.pdf) and US Census Bureau, Historical Marital Status Tables (census.gov/data/tables/time-series/demo/families/marital.html).
[2] From thepeoplehistory.com/1950.html & https://blog.cheapism.com/average-car-price-by-year/#slide=10.

Advertisement

Good thing he's grown

He seemed like a big fellow in the rush days of 1941. But it's a good thing he's bigger today. For the telephone system of nine years ago couldn't possibly do today's job.

Since 1941, the Bell System has increased the number of telephones by more than 16,000,000. There are nearly twice as many now as nine years ago.

Millions of miles of Long Distance circuits have been added. Billions of dollars have been spent for new equipment. The number of Bell Telephone employees has increased to more than 600,000.

Times like these emphasize the benefits of such growth and the value of a strong, healthy telephone company to serve the Nation's needs.

For now, more than ever, the Nation depends on telephone service to get things done and speed the job of defense.

BELL TELEPHONE SYSTEM

Advertisement

Pure-Pak...a New Horizon in everyday convenience!

Now you can say Goodbye Forever! to bottle washing, cash deposits and returns. Leading dairies in 47 states now sell top-quality milk in Pure-Pak...your personal milk container...used only once, only for dairy products, only by you...then tossed away like used food containers should be!

Milk is nature's finest food...and your food dollar's biggest buy. Milk in Pure-Pak saves nearly half the usual space–and it stays fresh and flavorful! Pure-Pak is the largest selling paper milk container in the world...nearly 300 million used every month! Ask for milk this *modern* way...*by name*...in Pure-Pak containers!

Pure-Pak   Your personal milk container

These words first appeared in print in the year 1950.

hot potato

BRAINWASHING

broad-spectrum

multimedia

deep fryer

off-the-shelf

epoxy resin

Private Label

Cardiac arrest

Ballistic Missile

bioengineering

SPIN OFF

shopping mall

Space shuttle

MUG SHOT

ACTION FIGURE

nail-biter

*From merriam-webster.com/time-traveler/1950.

A heartfelt plea from the author:

I sincerely hope you enjoyed reading this book and that it brought back many fond memories from the past.

Success as an author has become increasingly difficult with the proliferation of **AI generated** copycat books by unscrupulous sellers. They are clever enough to escape copyright action and use dark web tactics to secure paid-for **fake reviews**, something I would never do.

Hence I would like to ask you—I plead with you—the reader, to leave a star rating or review on Amazon. This helps make my book discoverable for new readers, and helps me to compete fairly against the devious copycats.

If this book was a gift to you, you can leave stars or a review on your own Amazon account, or you can ask the gift-giver or a family member to do this on your behalf.

I have enjoyed researching and writing this book for you and would greatly appreciate your feedback.

Best regards,
Bernard Bradforsand-Tyler.

Please leave a
book review/rating at:

https://bit.ly/1950-reviews

Or scan the QR code:

Flashback books make the perfect gift- see the full range at

https://bit.ly/FlashbackSeries

Image Attributions

Photographs and images used in this book are reproduced courtesy of the following:

Page 6 – From *Life* Magazine 27th Mar 1950.
Source: books.google.com/books?id=BFMEAAAAMBAJ&printsec (PD image).*
Page 8 – From *LOOK* Magazine Photograph Collection. Source: Library of Congress, Prints & Photographs Division, [Reproduction number e.g., LC-L9-60-8812, frame 8]. (PD image).*
Page 9 – From the Benjamin Moore House Paint 1950s advertisement. (PD image).*
Page 10 – Advertisement source: eBay.com. Pre 1978, no copyright mark (PD image).
Page 11 – Westinghouse advert, source: eBay.com. Pre 1978 no copyright mark (PD image). – Magazine by Science Service Inc. Source: comicbookplus.com/?cbplus=atomic. Pre 1978, no mark (PD image).
Page 12 – Advertisement source: loc.gov/pictures/item/2004668529/ (PD image).
Page 13 – Victoria Embankment j/w Westminster Bridge by Leonard Bentley. Source: search.creative commons.org/ photos/3d631476-f436-4609-86b4-875edda5c618. License CC BY-SA 2.0 (PD image).
Page 14 – British children in class. Creator unknown. Pre 1978, no copyright mark (PD image).
Page 15 – Advertisement source: eBay.com. Pre 1978, no copyright mark (PD image).
Page 16 – Photo source: digital.library.temple.edu/digital/collection/p15037coll3/id/61595. US government owned image. Photographer unknown, (PD image).
Page 17 – Advertisement source: eBay.com. Pre 1978, no copyright mark (PD image).
Page 18 – From *Life* Magazine 24th Apr 1950.
Source: books.google.com/books?id=oUkEAAAAMBAJ&printsec. (PD image).*
Page 19 – Ad source: flickr.com/photos/tom-margie/1441181992. Attribution 2.0 Generic (CC BY 2.0).
Page 20 – From *Life* Magazine 16th Oct 1950.
Source: books.google.com/books?id=CEwEAAAAMBAJ&printsec. (PD image).*
Page 21 – Studio promotional photo of Ed Sullivan. Source: the United States Library of Congress's Prints and Photographs division under the digital ID cph.3c23391. (PD image). –*The Lone Ranger* promotional photo from ABC Television April 11, 1960. Pre 1978, no copyright mark (PD image).
Page 22 – From *Life* Magazine 16th Oct 1950.
Source: books.google.com/books?id=CEwEAAAAMBAJ&printsec. (PD image).*
Page 23 – Promotional poster for *The Bob Hope Show*.** Source: loc.gov/exhibits/bobhope/tv. – Ralph Byrd promotional photo.** Source: historiasdecinema.com/2010/09/lembrando-grandes-seriados-2. – George Fenneman and Groucho Marx from the radio version of *You Bet Your Life* by NBC Radio. Source: commons.wikimedia.org/wiki/File:George_Fenneman_and_Groucho_Marx_You_Bet_Your_ Life_1951.jpg (PD image). – Jack Benny promotional photo from MCA.**
Source: commons.wikimedia.org/wiki/File:Jack_ Benny_and_vault.JPG.
Page 24 – Photo by Roger Higgins,1965 World Telegram staff photographer, donated to the United States Library of Congress's Prints and Photographs division the digital ID cph.3f06148.
Source: commons.wikimedia.org/wiki/File: Charles_Schulz_NYWTS.jpg (PD image).
Pages 24 & 25 – Reproductions of *Charlie Brown and Gang*. Reproductions are included here for information only under U.S. fair use laws due to: 1- No free alternative can exist of trademarked characters; 2- images are low resolution copies; 3- this does not limit the copyright owner's rights to sell the comic strip in any way; 4- Copies are too small to be used to make illegal copies for another book; 5- The images are significant to the article created.
Page 26 – Advert source: flickr.com/photos/tom-margie/1415323095/. Attribution-ShareAlike 2.0 Generic (CC BY-SA 2.0).
Page 27 – Advertisement source: restaurant-ingthroughhistory.com. Pre 1978, no copyright mark (PD image). – Diners Card photo. Photographer unknown. Source: economic-definition.com/Financial/ Kreditnaya_karta_ Credit_card__eto.html. Creator unknown. Pre 1978, no copyright mark (PD image).
Page 28 – Soviet poster, 1950.** Source: votefraud.org/josef_stalin_vote_fraud_page.htm. – Bulgarian poster, 1950.** Source: foreignmovieposters.tumblr.com/post/145135462086/liberated-china-1950-bulgarian-poster. – Sino-Soviet posters, 1950.** Source: cccpism.com/book/zhongsu/pic.htm.
Page 29 – Ivy Mike by The Official CTBTO, source: flickr.com/photos/ctbto/6476282811/. (PD image).
Page 30 – Compilation headlines from newspapers, 1950.
Page 31 – US tank and crew, source: commons.wikimedia.org/wiki/File:HA-SC-98-06983-Crew_of_M24 _along_Naktong_River_front-Korean_war-17_Aug_1950.JPEG. Camera Operator: SGT. RILEY. US Federal Government owned (PD image). – US soldiers photo source: commons.wikimedia.org/wiki/File: KoreanWarFallenSoldier1.jpg. Image by U.S. Army, US Federal Government owned (PD image).
– Chinese tanks photo. Source: forum.worldoftanks.ru. Creator unknown, Pre 1978 no mark (PD image).
Page 32 – Allied army in Korea photos source: commons.wikimedia.org/wiki/Category:United_States_ Army_in_the_Korean_War. Crown copyright work owned by the Australian Government. Photographer unknown, (PD image). – Canadian army, source: i.dailymail.co.uk/i/newpix/2018/05/31/20/ 4CCA9CBB00000578-5789731 -image-a-20_1527795199977.jpg.

– British army in Korea photos, source: home.bt.com/news/on-this-day/june-25-1950-invasion-from-communist-north-sparks-the-start-of-the-korean-war-11363988570216. Crown copyright owned by the British Government. Creator unknown (PD image).
Page 33 – From *Life* Magazine 24th Apr 1950.
Source: books.google.com/books?id=oUkEAAAAMBAJ&printsec. (PD image).*
Page 34 – Photos: sahistory.org.za/article/group-areas-act-1950, and religiousleftlaw.com/2014/04/index.html photographers unknown. Pre 1978, no copyright mark (PD image).
Page 35 – Danger sign, from a farm sign in Johannesburg. 1st July 1952. Source: commons.wikimedia.org/wiki/Category:Apartheid_signage Pre 1978, no copyright mark (PD image). – Caution sign, source: fr.igihe.com/IMG/ arton16496.jpg?1451940393, creator unknown. Pre 1978, no mark (PD image).
Page 36 – Indian Stamp, 1950. Source: commons.wikimedia.org/wiki/File:1950_Republic_India_04.jpg (PD image). – Street procession: merepix.com/2013/01/india-first-republic-day-celebrations-jan-26-1950-photos.html photographer unknown. Pre 1978, no copyright mark (PD image).
Page 37 – Joseph McGinnis, 1956. Source: fbi.gov/history/famous-cases/brinks-robbery. Pre 1978, no copyright mark (PD image). – Mug shots of the Brinks robbers, 1956. Source: robertallisonhistory.wordpress.com/2020/04/16/the-brinks-robber-crime-of-the-century/. Pre 1978, no mark (PD image).
Page 38 – Advertisement source: ebay.ie. Pre 1978, no copyright mark (PD image).*
Page 39 – TWA poster, 1950.** Source: commons.wikimedia.org/wiki/File:TWA_Italy_Poster_(18857334053).jpg. – Northwest Airlines poster, 1950.** Source: vintageadbrowser.com/airlines-and-aircraft-ads-1950s/7. – Air France poster, 1950.** Source: flickr.com/photos/estampemoderne/5842503124. Attribution-NoDerivs 2.0 Generic (CC BY-ND 2.0).
– Air Liban poster, 1950.** Source: en.artprecium.com/images/photos/21/5c8273b4dc6bf.jpg.
Page 40 – Still image from the film *The Men*, 1950.** Source: imdb.com. – A Streetcar Named Desire 1951 film poster.** Source: en.wikipedia.org/wiki/A_Streetcar_Named_ Desire_(1951_film).
Page 41 – Still image from the film *The Wild One*, 1953.** Source: kinopoisk.ru/picture/1947898/.
– Still image from the film *Marc Anthony*, 1950.** Source: flickr.com/photos/jumborois/3354472656/.
– Still image from the film *The Godfather*, 1972.** Source: en.wikipedia.org/wiki/Vito_Corleone.
– Still image from the film *On the Waterfront*, 1954.**
Source: flickr.com/photos/classicvintage/9316236341. Attribution 4.0 International (CC BY 4.0).
Page 42 – Still image from the film *Fancy Pants, 1950*.** Source: imdb.com. – *Rio Grande* publicity still. Source: commons.wikimedia.org/wiki/Category: Rio_Grande_(film). Permission PD-US no copyright notice. (PD image). – Monroe publicity photo.
Source: commons.wikimedia.org/wiki/File:Monroe_1953_publicity.jpg (PD image).
Page 43 – 1950 *Cinderella* film poster.** Source: commons.wikimedia.org/wiki/Category:Cinderella_(1950_film). – 1950 *Father of the Bride* poster.** Source: wikivisually.com/wiki/File:FatheroftheBride 1950.jpg. – *King Solomon's Mines* 1950 poster.** Source: flickr.com/photos/jumborois/2816930851/.
Page 44 – Movie posters from 1950 for: *Spy Hunt* by Universal Pictures.** *Guilty of Treason* by Freedom Productions.** *I Married a Communist* by RKO.** and *Destination Moon* by George Pal Productions.**
All movie posters source: rottentomatoes.com.
Page 45 – From *Life* Magazine 16th Oct 1950.
Source: books.google.com/books?id=CEwEAAAAMBAJ&printsec. (PD image).*
Page 46 – Guys and Dolls theatrical poster from 1950.** Source: upload.wikimedia.org/wikipedia/commons/c/cc/Guys-and-Dolls-Original-Poster.jpg. Attribution-ShareAlike 4.0 International (CC BY-SA 4.0). – Promotional stage photo. Source: fanpix.famousfix.com/gallery/robert-alda/p101956377. Pre 1978, no mark (PD image). – 1955 Cinema poster .** Source: famousfix.com/topic/guys-and-dolls.
Page 47 – *The Lion the Witch and the Wardrobe* book cover and *Narnia* film posters.**
Source: en.wikipedia.org/wiki/The_Lion,_the_Witch_and_the_Wardrobe.
Page 48 – From *Life* Magazine 28th Aug 1950.
Source: books.google.com/books?id=Dk4EAAAAMBAJ&printsec
Page 49 – Patti Page source: wikivisually.com/wiki/Patti_Page by General Artists Corporation (management). Permission PD-PRE1978 (PD image).
– Nat King Cole in 1952, source: commons.wikimedia.org/wiki/Category:Nat_King_Cole by GAC-General Artists Corporation (management). Permission PD-PRE1978 (PD image).
Page 50 – Guy Lombardo in 1944. Source: wikivisually.com/wiki/Guy_Lombardo from Music Corporation of America-photo by Maurice Seymour, Chicago. Permission PD-PRE1978 (PD image).
– Gordon Jenkin, creator unkown. Source: imdb.com/name/nm0420851/?ref_=nm_mv_close.
– Sammy Kaye source: wikivisually.com/wiki/Sammy_Kaye by MCA-Music Corporation of America; photographer: James Kriegsmann, New York Permission PD-PRE1978 (PD image). – Kay Starr, studio publicity photo, Source: en.wikipedia.org/wiki/Kay_Starr. Pre 1978, no copyright mark (PD image).
Page 51 – Perry Como by NBC Television, 1956. Source: commons.wikimedia.org/wiki/File:Perry_

Como_1956.JPG. Permission PD-PRE1978 (PD image). – Bing Crosby. Source: commons.wikimedia.org/wiki/File:Bing_Crosby,_1942. jpg. Creative Commons CC0 1.0 Universal Public Domain Dedication.
Page 52 – Advert source: flickr.com/photos/vintageimagenook/28713746517/. Public Domain Mark 1.0
Page 53 – Print advertisement for Frederick's of Hollywood. Pre 1978, no copyright mark (PD image).
Page 54 – Fashion magazine covers from 1951. Pre 1978, no copyright mark (PD image).
Page 55 – Advert source: imgur.com/gallery/F6UwKM2. Pre 1978, no copyright mark (PD image).
Page 56 – Photo by Lars Nordin, CC BY 4.0, Source: commons.wikimedia.org/w/index.php?curid=39208366. Licensed under Creative Commons Attribution 4.0 International.
Page 57 – Jantzen advert. Source: flickr.com/photos/nesster/5521936717/. Attrib 4.0 Int (CC BY 4.0)
Page 58 – Marilyn Monroe in 1952 studio publicity portrait for film Niagara, by 20th Century Fox. (PD image). – Models walking photo. Source: Jessica at myvintagevogue.com. Licensed under CC BY 2.0.
Page 59 – Sinatra, source: morrisonhotelgallery.com/collections/wtvp8g/The-Sinatra-Experience-. – Brando, source: dailybreak.co/wp-content/uploads/2019/06/Marlon-Brando-Ford-Thunderbird-1955-Est.-2444.jpg. – Dean, source: en.wikipedia.org/wiki/James_Dean. All images this page Pre-1978, no copyright mark (PD image).
Page 60 – Advert source: flickr.com/photos/nesster/5514151747/. Attribution 4.0 Internat (CC BY 4.0).
Page 61 – From *Life* Magazine 27th Mar 1950.
Source: books.google.com/books?id=BFMEAAAAMBAJ&printsec. (PD image).*
Page 62 – 1950 Trade advertisement for an Australian documentary. Source: tutorversal.com/blog/xxi-commonwealth-games-2018-the-story-so-far.html. Pre 1978, no copyright mark (PD image).
Page 63 – Photograph by BRDC/Silverstone Experience. Source: welt.de/sport/formel1/plus207948105/70-Jahre-Formel-1-Waehrend-meiner-Karriere-starben-65-Fahrer.html. – 1950 Poster. Source: progcovers.com/motor/ montecarlo.html. Permission PD-PRE1978 (PD image). – Guiseppe Farina. Source: dummysports.com/1950-f1/. Photographer unknown. Pre 1978, no copyright mark (PD image).
Page 64 – From *Life* Magazine 24th April 1950.
Source: books.google.com/books?id=oUkEAAAAMBAJ&printsec. (PD image).*
Page 65 – Advertisement by Liggett & Myers Tobacco Company, 1950. Source: Stanford Research into the Impact of Tobacco Advertising, (PD image).
Page 66 – Demaret, source: golfhistorytoday.com/jimmy-demaret-born-1910/. Pre 1978, no mark (PD image). – Cooper, source: basketball.fandom.com/wiki/Chuck_Cooper. Pre 1978, no mark (PD image).
Page 67 – Kübler, source: capovelo.com/oldest-living-tour-de-france-winner-ferdinand-ferdi-kubler-dies/. Creator unknown. Pre 1978, no copyright mark (PD image). – Toweel, source: alchetron.com/Vic-Toweel. Creator unknown. Pre 1978, no copyright mark (PD image).
Page 68 – Harry Truman, Source: Library of Congress's Prints and Photographs division under the digital ID cph 3c17122 (PD image). – Albert Einstein, Source: Library of Congress's Prints and Photographs division under the digital ID cph.3b46036 (PD image).
Page 69 – Smoking women, creator unknown. Pre 1978, no copyright mark (PD image). – Shirley Temple, source: uk.wikipedia.org/wiki/Ширлі_Темпл. Pre 1978, no copyright mark (PD image). – James Dean Studio promotional photo, source: af.wikipedia.org/wiki/James_Dean#/media/Lêer:James_Dean_ca_1955.jpg. Pre 1978, no copyright mark (PD image).
Page 70 – Advertisement source: imgur.com/gallery/GQ8T4. Pre 1978, no copyright mark (PD image).
Page 71 – Advert source: flickr.com/photos/dok1/8583523120/. Attribution 4.0 Internat (CC BY 4.0).
Page 72-74 – All photos are, where possible, CC BY 2.0 or PD images made available by the creator for free use including commercial use. Where commercial use photos are unavailable, photos are included here for information only under U.S. fair use laws due to: 1- images are low resolution copies; 2- images do not devalue the ability of the copyright holders to profit from the original works in any way; 3- Images are too small to be used to make illegal copies for use in another book; 4- The images are relevant to the article created.
Page 75 – From *Life* Magazine 27th Mar 1950.
Source: books.google.com/books?id=BFMEAAAAMBAJ&printsec. (PD image).*
Page 78 & 79 – From *Life* Mag 25th Sep and *Life* Mag 16th Oct 1950, sources: books.google.com/books?id=6OoEAAAAMBAJ&source & books.google.com/books?id=CEwEAAAAMBAJ&printsec. (PD images).*

*Advertisement (or image from an advertisement) is in the public domain because it was published in a collective work (such as a periodical issue) in the US between 1925 and 1977 and without a copyright notice specific to the advertisement.
**Posters for movies or events are either in the public domain (published in the US between 1925 and 1977 and without a copyright notice specific to the artwork) or owned by the production company, creator, or distributor of the movie or event. Posters, where not in the public domain, and screen stills from movies or TV shows, are reproduced here under USA Fair Use laws due to: 1- images are low resolution copies; 2- images do not devalue the ability of the copyright holders to profit from the original works in any way; 3- Images are too small to be used to make illegal copies for use in another book; 4- The images are relevant to the article created.

This book was written by Bernard Bradforsand-Tyler as part of *A Time Traveler's Guide* series of books.

All rights reserved. The author exerts the moral right to be identified as the author of the work.

No parts of this book may be reproduced, stored in any retrieval system, or transmitted in any form or by any means, without prior written permission from the author.

This is a work of nonfiction. No names have been changed, no events have been fabricated. The content of this book is provided as a source of information for the reader, however it is not meant as a substitute for direct expert opinion. Although the author has made every effort to ensure that the information in this book is correct at time of printing, and while this publication is designed to provide accurate information in regard to the subject matters covered, the author assumes no responsibility for errors, inaccuracies, omissions, or any other inconsistencies herein and hereby disclaims any liability to any party for any loss, damage, or disruption caused by errors or omissions.

All images contained herein are reproduced with the following permissions:
- Images included in the public domain.
- Images obtained under creative commons license.
- Images included under fair use terms.
- Images reproduced with owner's permission.

All image attributions and source credits are provided at the back of the book. All images are the property of their respective owners and are protected under international copyright laws.

First printed in 2020 in the USA (ISBN 979-8665386867).
Revised in 2021, 2nd Ed (ISBN 978-645062304)
& 2024, 3rd Ed (ISBN 978-1-922676-27-6).
Self-published by B. Bradforsand-Tyler.

www.ingramcontent.com/pod-product-compliance
Lightning Source LLC
Chambersburg PA
CBHW070320120526
44590CB00017B/2761